BENTLEY
Heritage

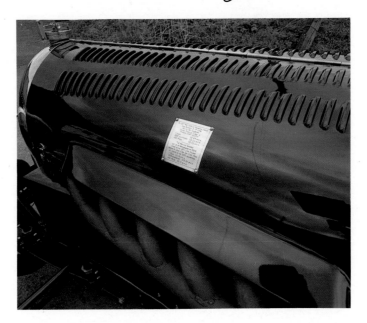

BENTLEY
Heritage

RICHARD BIRD

First published in 1991 by
Osprey Publishing Limited
59 Grosvenor Street London W1X 9DA

Cataloguing in Publication Data for this title
is available from the British Library

ISBN 1 85532 187 4

Editor Shaun Barrington
Page design Angela Posen
Printed in Hong Kong

About the author
Richard Bird has been a professional
photographer for 25 years. His
clients include Toyota and Honda
Motorcycles. As an admirer of
British innovation and
workmanship, this book was, for
'Dickie' Bird, a labour of love.

Half title page
*Bentley 8-litre which was still
breaking records more than 50 years
after it was built*

Title page
*Driven by F C Clement and Richard
Watney, this Speed Six covered 1,760
miles in the 24-hour Grand Prix
d'Endurance. The result was a Bentley
one-two, with Glen Kidston and Woolf
Barnato taking the laurels*

Right
*Mulliner-bodied 6½-litre, the second
production 6½ built, now in Vermont,
USA. Still totally original*

For a catalogue of all books published by Osprey Automotive
please write to:

**The Marketing Department, Octopus Illustrated Books,
1st Floor, Michelin House, 81 Fulham Road, London SW3 6RB**

Contents

Introduction and Acknowledgements

This book is a pictorial record (or perhaps more accurately, a celebration) of those 1920s Bentleys that are in existence today. It is difficult to be confident of production figures, but between 1919 and 1931, Bentley Motors produced some 3024 cars. A few experimental designs and oddities increase the (disputed) total to 3039. Of these, some 1600 are known to survive: and most of these – their very survival a tribute to the engineering skills and craftsmanship of their creators – are not museum pieces. They are driven, and driven hard: in sprints, hillclimbs, time-trials, rallies, or if not run in competition, then they cover endless miles as 'regular' transport (at least as regular as a 1920s Bentley could ever be).

You will find these vintage machines not just in England or Europe, but in the United States, in India, South Africa and Australia; wherever someone has been seduced by engineering excellence or dreams of Le Mans glory days.

At the risk of stating the obvious to any Bentley owner, one of the joys of these cars – particularly for a photographer – is that they were made in the era of the coachbuilder, when a customer would order a chassis from Bentley Motors and then could choose the body almost à la carte (though admittedly there were standard bodies available from Vanden Plas, Hoopers, Park Ward *et al* – and most 1920s Bentleys received a Vanden Plas body through the Bentley Company). Nevertheless, the variety of coachwork, and the myriad decisions that the customer could make concerning lamps, instrumentation and trim, mean that every early Bentley is unique.

The multiplicity of styles on the chassis of the 3-litre, 4½-litre, 6½-litre, Speed Six and 8-litre which feature in these pages has an effect – mostly a liberating effect – on restoration parameters today. If the original owners were sending their cars to be heavily plated, or ordering paint finishes more or less in any colours they wished, then who is to say just exactly how a 'standard' 1920s Bentley should look? There is no right and wrong as to the extent of restoration work, only personal preference.

Vanden Plas-bodied car of the mid 1930s. Five Bentleys were built more or less to this style under the supervision of 'Nobby' Clarke, the man who built the first Bentley engine and who was race team manager from 1927 onwards

Above
Works-built 1926 Le Mans 3-litre.
This car, photographed in Kensington
Gardens in 1990, is in almost perfectly
original condition. Despite the
dilapidated state of the upholstery and
the so-so paintwork, to some
enthusiasts, restoration might
spell ruination

Opposite
Similar styling to YM83, with no
stoneguard to the radiator. The small
dome on the front wheel backplate
indicates that this car has been fitted
with the later self-wrapping braking
system designed by the Bentley
company

Some of the photographs in this book have been taken at the main events in the vintage Bentley calendar – the concours meeting in Kensington and the annual August racing at Silverstone, both organised by the Bentley Drivers' Club – and at various local rallies. There are pictures of the genuine Le Mans team cars and of the 'Blower' Bentleys. The work of professional restorers is featured, together with an intriguing look at the current state of some of the greatest stars, such as 'Bluebell', 'Old Number One' and 'Old Mother Gun'. It is hoped that the pictures reproduced here will show these magnificent motor cars to be not only fascinating examples of engineering excellence from a bygone era, but also as infectiously driveable sporting machines, perfectly able to cope with modern road conditions after more than sixty years.

The author and publishers would like to thank all those who graciously presented their cars for photography, and the restorers who allowed such disruption of their workshops and showrooms. In particular, Tessa and David Llewellyn, Elizabeth and David McDonald, Rosemary and Bill Lake, Anne and Brian Hamilton, Norris Kennard, John Otto-Jones, Diana Barnato, Stanley Mann, Dick Moss, Ivan Dutton, Gordon Russell of Elmdown Vintage Autos, Coys the auctioneers and Bill Port and Barbara Fell of the Bentley Drivers' Club. Special thanks to Len Wilton, without whose organising efforts and enthusiasm this book would not exist.

Left
*The unusual rear styling of a late
1920s Doctor's coupé. The height
indicates Gurney Nutting coachwork*

Above
*65 years old and quite capable of
handling today's not quite so open
road*

A brief History of Bentley, 1919–1931

In a book of this nature, which is essentially a photographic record of vintage Bentleys alive and kicking today, there is of course space enough only for the briefest of resumés of the Bentley story. There are many books available on the subject; one of the most shrewd and revealing being Michael Frostick's *Bentley: Cricklewood to Crewe* (Osprey, 1980). For the atmosphere of the company and the times, *Bentley Past and Present* by Rivers Fletcher (Gentry Books Ltd, 1982) is recommended; and for the mechanics, *Technical Facts of the Vintage Bentley* produced by the Bentley Drivers' Club.

Walter Owen Bentley was born in 1888, the ninth child of a wealthy Yorkshire family residing in Hampstead, London. He left Clifton College in Bristol at the age of 16 and became an apprentice for three years at the Great Northern Railway Works in Doncaster. The temptation to speculate as to the importance of this experience – particularly when looking at the rounded scuttle of a prototype 3-litre, or when confronted by the sheer mass of the later 8-litre powerplant – is almost irresistible. But two things must surely have happened to the young public schoolboy: the first is the acquisition of a basic grounding in metallurgy; the second is a rude awakening to the realities of the world of work.

Leaving the railway works, W O worked for the National Motor Cab Company in London. Then, at the age of 24, it was down to business for real. With part of their inheritance, W O and his brother H M (Hardy) bought the company of Lecoq and Fernie, importers of three French makes of motor car, most importantly, the DFP. Before the Great War intervened to bring trading for the new firm of Bentley and Bentley Ltd to a temporary close, W O had the French fit aluminium pistons to a 12/15. On the strength of this revolutionary (and successful) innovation, W O spent the war refining and designing aero-engines. Whilst at Humber in Coventry, he met F T Burgess and worked with him on the successful BR 1 and BR 2 aero-engines. It was in conjunction with Burgess that the first Bentley was designed: the new 3-litre engine was first tested in a room above the DFP service station in October 1919, less than a year after the Armistice. That engine was the basis for the car W O had wanted to build right from the start: a reliable unit that could power a fast tourer over long

Special windscreen pillars and door treatment on this ivory 3-litre with its burnished aluminium bonnet

The Corner brothers' 3-litre is a common sight around Bromley in Kent; to the purists, the 3-litre is the Bentley, untrammelled by customer demands, a direct expression of W O's vision

distances with the minimum of maintenance (not, it should be noted, a racing machine).

Very soon, the nucleus of the group of engineers and racing drivers that came to be known as the 'Bentley Boys' was formed. Clive Gallop (who had links with Peugeot and had worked for Aston Martin pre-war) worked on the camshafts, 'Nobby' Clarke actually built the first engine; and Wally Hassan joined as a 16-year-old apprentice.

To unravel where the money came from for the new factory at Cricklewood, for paying suppliers and men and running the showrooms, would take up the rest of this book. W O managed not only to design and sell the 3-litre, but also to design the 6½-litre, with a gaggle of investors, no firm capital base and a whole mess of mortgages, before millionaire racer Capt. Woolf Barnato intervened in 1926. The company was then liquidated and reformed and all the original £1 shares were devalued to one shilling. The injection of the Captain's capital ensured the survival of the company until 1931.

Despite the financial precariousness of the company, over 1600 3-litre Bentleys were made. The car was first introduced in *The Autocar* in November 1919 (an ecstatic review the like of which is very rarely seen today, with talk of pulse quickening and the 'dark unattainable line of the horizon'). One of the joys of the first Bentley is that W O could not have been burdened either by the knowledge of what his competitors were producing – because he started work so soon after the Great War – nor of what his customers would be looking for – because this was his first effort and there was no obvious customer profile. What he (and the Bentley team) produced was what *they* wanted – a fast tourer with a reliable chassis and a robust engine built individually by one fitter and his mate; 4-cylinder ohc with plenty enough power for the open bodies provided by various coachbuilders. As demand for enclosed, heavier, coachwork increased however, the need for more power meant a bigger engine – initially the $6\frac{1}{2}$, and then an engine based open the 6-cylinder block

Sporting four-seater 3-litre in Kensington; a suitable location for one of the most elegant of British motor cars

15

Above
Flared wings, four doors and a three-piece windscreen on this grey 3-litre. Lots of Bentleys were originally grey

Right
Standard-looking 3-litre with Vanden Plas bodywork; the engine was considered 'medium sized and economical' back in the 1920s

(minus two cylinders), the $4\frac{1}{2}$. The pictures in this book should not mislead you: most $4\frac{1}{2}$s and $6\frac{1}{2}$s were in fact given saloon/limousine bodies.

The $6\frac{1}{2}$-litre's great feature was its overhead camshaft, made possible by the design of a three-throw eccentric shaft of specially hardened steel. The complexity of this camshaft drive meant that the engines took much longer than the $4\frac{1}{2}$s to be assembled and tested at Oxgate Lane, Cricklewood. Its 140 bhp (at 3200 rpm) could more easily cope with, say, the limousine bodies from Gurney Nutting or the saloon coachwork from Freestone and Webb. First introduced in 1925, more than 350 $6\frac{1}{2}$s were built.

The $6\frac{1}{2}$-litre brochure contains this caveat: 'Purchasers of Bentley chassis to which coachwork is to be fitted other than to the Company's order should ensure that the coachbuilders rigidly adhere to the detailed bodybuilder's instructions issued by the Company with each chassis, as a certain amount of inconvenience both to the owners and to the Company has been caused in the past by neglect in this direction. This was a very real problem noted by Rivers Fletcher (in *Bentley Past and Present*), at that time a young Bentley apprentice. There was never any problem with open Vanden Plas sports bodies nor from H J Mulliner standard saloons, or coachwork from Hoopers or Park Ward. But many other coachbuilders made terrible mistakes, such as not leaving enough room for full travel of the springs or blocking the steering lock.

The 6-cylinder 6½ was well received by the carriage trade, and most bodies put on the long chassis – such as the Barker boat-tail, all swooping wings and burnished aluminium – were 'Grand Touring' at its best. But the sporting clientele, some of whom had bought the 3-litre, (finally discontinued in 1929) were looking for a second generation sporting model. The 4½-litre was the answer. The 4½ was modified over the years, but what it had from the beginning (1927), it retained: a handbuilt engine which gave 20 bhp more than the 3-litre – actually this is Bentley's own figure – the reality was probably double – with valves that didn't need decarbonising for 20,000 miles, which was at ease (indeed happiest) cruising at 60 mph over long distances; and the same well-balanced 3-litre chassis (wheelbase 117.5 or 130 in) with a five-year guarantee. A sporting 1928 four-seater with fabric-covered body (the fashion was for fabric) would cost you £1,295. A Weymann saloon was £1,150. Even if a customer ordered a standard four-light or open sports body, there was still a choice of colour and upholstery, and decisions to be made about lamps, plating and instrumentation; so that (as the photographs in this book demonstrate) every car was unique.

One famous option was the 'Semi Le Mans' model, or Le Mans Replica: a quick action filler for the larger fuel tank, a stoneguard built into the radiator, large rev counter, harder suspension with double shock absorbers and Bentley racing green finish all came as part of the package. (It is impossible to tell much of the 1920s Bentley production models story without talking about racing.)

1929 saw the production of the famous supercharged 4½s, the Bentley Blowers, the fulfilment of Sir Henry 'Tim' Birkin's dream of racing such a machine at Le Mans. W O strongly disapproved of the modification, believing that it would adversely affect the durability and handling of his creation, a misgiving that was largely vindicated when the cars actually entered competition. Tim Birkin was not to be denied, and (with Capt. Barnato's backing) 55 cars were built with Amherst Villiers superchargers. The rules on homologation for Le Mans required a minimum of 50 production models to be built. Despite the extra thickness of the radiator core, the cars ran hot in traffic – and even hotter at Le Mans and Brooklands . . . But there could be no denying the excitement of that surge of power.

The Speed Six was introduced in the same year. Unlike the Blower Bentleys, W O's heart was in this development of the original 6½-litre. The high compression engine with twin carburettors on a shorter chassis could (and did) blow the Blowers away over distance, though top speed was lower. Production 'run' for the 'Silent Speed Six' is quoted as 181 – far fewer than for the original 6½ or the 4½. The

The brown 3-litre with the 4½s is a reminder that 'colour of body and upholstery [were] according to the customer's choice' (3-litre catalogue)

Des Williams' 3-litre, an unusual brown finish, pictured at home

Bentley brochure pointed out the car's 'suitability for the owner driver'; and there is no denying that the handling of the car was – and is – responsive and refined, the extra power coming to the rescue of those without a chauffeur's deftness with the clutch and the 18-in steering wheel.

By 1930 – post-Wall Street Crash – receivership was only a few months away; but W O still had one masterpiece to unveil before the Bentley history becomes part of Rolls-Royce history and outside the scope of this book. The last great 'independent' Bentley was the 8-litre leviathan. As to the chassis, the massive tubular cross members and deep side rails were assembled in close consultation with the coachbuilders, whose work would be vital to the success of the model. The gearbox was redesigned for the 8-litre, and this and the extra power again made for a car which not only performed magnificently, but was actually a relatively pliant machine to drive, capable of 100-mph plus with even the heaviest limousine coachwork. Most 8-litres weighed in at around 50 or 60 cwt. *The Motor* tested W O's own 8-litre (GK 706) at Brooklands in December. Over the half-mile it was timed at 101.12 mph, which annoyed everyone in the Bentley workshops considerably, because the car had been touching 110 mph without too much trouble a few days earlier!

Whilst there was nothing revolutionary about the powerplant – quite rightly, following the principle that if ain't broke, don't fix it – it retained all the excellence of its predecessors: four valves per cylinder, overhead camshaft, 8-bearing crankshaft, two spark plugs per cylinder, twin carbs, and, above all, superb build quality. A team of 8-litres would never race at Le Mans – time was up for Bentley

John Otto-Jones' 3-litre at home in Cardiff. It should not be forgotten when contemplating the sometimes stately lines of the Bentley (particularly those with later, heavier coachwork) that these cars were world-class endurance racers from the very beginning. A standard four-seater secured the 24-hour record, the 'Double Twelve' at Brooklands on September 27/28, 1922: 2082 miles, at an average speed of 86.79 mph, as reported in Bentley's own publication – and of course the Le Mans glory days were still to come . . .

YP 5494

Motors even before the car was released anyway, but that wasn't the reason for not tilting for yet another victory in 1931. The car was supposed to be competing with the big Rolls-Royce in the luxury closed car market: racing was not the right image. Approximately 100 of these magnificent cars were built. The chassis cost £1,850 in 1930.

Before the fateful date of 11 July, 1931, when the receiver was appointed and Bentley ceased to trade, there was one more model released. In an effort to survive by attracting customers to a smaller car and compete with the Rolls-Royce 20/25, Bentley produced the 4-litre. The engine – while perfectly serviceable – was not to W O's design, with overhead inlet valves, a completely 'foreign' combustion chamber shape and only one sparking plug per cylinder. What was worse, was that this unit was married to the massive 8-litre chassis. This was a sure sign that the writing was on the wall: a case of 'buy now while stocks last'. Just 50 of these cars were built. In less than a decade, Bentley had acquired a reputation for producing sporting motor cars and tourers to match any in the world – this wasn't one of them. Far better, therefore, not to dwell upon it, but to consider what really made Bentley tick. . . .

The epitome of the standard 3-litre Bentley tourer, from its barrel-shaped door hinges to its cream and brown livery

Right and below
*Richard Moss's 6½-litre special.
The overall weight and frontal area
have been reduced, increasing
performance quite significantly.
Richard is well-known for his
meticulous restoration work*

Richard Moss and his team restored this 6½-litre over two years. 363 6½-litres were built; actual displacement is 6597 cc

Left
A brace of 4½-litres and a 3-litre, all in black. Top speed for the 'standard' 3-litre was just over 80 mph (as tested by The Motor, March 1925); the 4½ offered genuine 100-mph performance

Above
Meticulously restored 4½-litre, graceful with the hood up; the 4½ engine block was 100 × 140 mm, compared to the 3-litre's 80 × 149 mm

Above
David McDonald (left) is the owner of the black Le Mans 4½-litre pictured. Just over 700 4½-litre Bentleys were produced

Left and above
Supremely elegant $4\frac{1}{2}$-litre; the side shot emphasises the commanding driving position, in the dead centre of the car. This is a 'two seat plus dicky'. The fully enclosed cover for the spare wheel is unusual

The purposeful sporting lines of a perfect 4½-litre. The owner, Gibbs Pancheri, is on the right. 'The Company has experienced a demand for a larger model' explained the catalogue, 'a car which will earn the right to be called the leader of all sports cars' . . . The screen makes an excellent wine tray

4½-litre with the hood up: a rare sight

Heading for home in a 4½. 'The 4½-litre chassis, in common with other Bentley models, carries a five year guarantee. This is unique in that sports models are not generally supposed to have a very long life.' (From the Bentley catalogue)

Above
Len Wilton in a $4\frac{1}{2}$-litre Le Mans
model with cycle wings. The model
actually came after the $6\frac{1}{2}$-litre, the
$6\frac{1}{2}$ first released in 1925, the $4\frac{1}{2}$ in
1927

Right
$4\frac{1}{2}$-litre Blower Bentley; in 1969, every
vintage Bentley with a sense of history
turned up at Le Mans to celebrate the
40th anniversary of the Bentley 1-2-3-
4 at the Sarthe circuit. This car was
there with owner John Zeal. The $4\frac{1}{2}$ is
still in perfect condition today

Previous page
Gratifyingly original black 4½ owned by John Otto-Jones. The lamps and overall bodywork are just right, though the tool box lacks a lid

Above
Note the differences between the standard 4½ and David McDonald's Le Mans 'replica' (behind). A harder suspension is the main technical difference

Right and overleaf
The modification that W O never wanted to see: the 'Blower' Bentleys. GY 7847 is seen her at Coys the auctioneers, looking for a new home. Supercharging the 4½ was the idea of Sir Henry ('Tim') Birkin, who wanted to race the blown Bentleys at Le Mans – which meant homologation and consequently the building of 50 of the cars

The Speed Six, a development of the former six-cylinder car; overhead camshaft, two carburettors, higher compression and a longer chassis

Replica team car Speed Six with 1929
Le Mans specifications

Previous page
This imposing Speed Six has just been put through its paces around Silverstone, which explains the wide grin. The body style is unique; in some ways all Bentleys are unique in that no two Bentleys ever drive the same, even with the same specifications and even after having been completely stripped and rebuilt

Above
W O Bentley's masterpiece, the 8-litre: 'the complete car has truly that mysterious quality which makes one forget that it is a machine at all.' (The Autocar, September 5, 1930)

The 8-litre dwarfs the onlookers, but its proportions are such that the car retains integrity. After 60 years, its power, quietness and general driveability are as impressive as ever

Above
Modified 8-litre sitting low in the water with mid-1930s Corsica body

Right
The last model produced by Bentley Motors, the 1931 4-litre; the coachwork is particularly attractive, but the engine is not to W O's design – pushrod with a separate cylinder head

The Racing

W O had prepared the DFP which he and his brother had been selling before the Great War for hillclimbs, on the more or less spurious grounds that the publicity would be useful; and that extremely questionable but often exploited argument that 'racing improves the breed'. Before that, he had been racing in TTs and winning trials on a Rex and other motorcycles as a teenager. There is no doubt that racing was in his blood from the very early years; and a consideration of the 1920s history of Bentley reveals that it begins and – for W O at least – ends, with racing. As the money situation worsened and others on the board had more and more of a say in the production activities of the company, no one contradicted W O when it came to the organisation of the race team.

That is not to imply that W O went racing with the company's money with his eyes closed: he always insisted that Bentley never entered a race unless they knew they could win. There is no doubt that success at Le Mans had an effect – albeit indeterminate – on the sales of the 3-litre, the $4\frac{1}{2}$ and the Speed Six; even if a Bentley owner had a heavy saloon body fitted to his chassis and used the car for Sunday picnics, he could still enjoy some vicarious pleasure in the dramas of the Sarthes circuit or at Brooklands.

The Bentley racing saga begins with EX2, Experimental Number 2 (the prototype that was the basis for much of the work which produced the 3-litre), at Brooklands in 1921. After one failure to start, it notched up the first Bentley win in a junior sprint handicap in May of that year.

The car was driven by Frank Clement, arguably to become the most important of the Bentley racing drivers by virtue of his position as a true professional, an employee of the company. His mechanical knowledge and intimate understanding of the Bentleys he drove meant that, according to those who saw him race, he never made a mistake.

Next outings were the Isle of Man Tourist Trophy in 1922, and, surprisingly, the Indianapolis 500. A single car went to the Indy, finished 13th, and gained an honourable mention in despatches – *Motor Age* – 'it would be unfair to the foreign contingent . . . not to give a word to the English Bentley Special'. Presumably the effort and expense of a transatlantic trip was considered worth the publicity. In the TT, the three Bentleys won the team prize and came second, fourth and fifth. The most notable fact about the race – apart from, of

The following pictures were taken at the Bentley Drivers Club meeting that takes place every year at Silverstone. None of the cars in the next half-dozen photographs in the paddock were actually competing. The chrome spokes on this superb 8-litre are unusually long; it must have been difficult to fit them to the rims. In fact, the wheels look more like Rolls-Royce than Bentley; just another example of customer preference

This two-seater 8-litre special is owned by Mike Wilcock, an RAC scrutineer, so there shouldn't be much wrong with it!

course, the team result and the excellent publicity garnered because all three cars were not far off standard models – was that W O raced himself; something the insurance companies would soon forbid.

In 1923, the French had an idea for a race which seemed a little crazy: 24 hours, through the night, for standard production cars. Could *any* car around survive such a test? Bentley tried it anyway, and gained a more than creditable fourth place in the first 24-hour Le Mans. Over the following years, Bentley became so closely associated with the endurance classic that one was unthinkable without the other. 1924 saw the first Bentley Le Mans victory, Capt. John Duff and Frank Clement the winning team. The next two years saw mechanical failure for all Bentley entrants and consequently pressure on W O to withdraw to avoid the adverse publicity which would inevitably come with a third wipe-out. But W O and the race team held out: and 1927 would be the first year of a sequence of four Bentley victories.

The Bentley 3-litre driven by motorsport journalist Sammy Davis and Dr J Benjafield won at an average speed of 61.36 mph; the fastest lap (73.01 mph) was achieved by Frank Clement in a $4\frac{1}{2}$. Behind the

bare bones, there lies an extraordinary story. In the semi-darkness at 9.30 pm, 5½ hours into the race, a six-car pile-up at White House Corner left Bentleys 1 and 2 unable to continue, and the eventual winner with twisted dumbirons and damaged front wing. Despite having to lash a pocket lamp to the windscreen to replace the smashed sidelamp, Bentley no. 3 chased after the Aries (which eventually broke under the strain on its 129th lap) to win by 212 miles. Dr Benjafield deserves a book all to himself, a courageous driver apparently with no mechanical comprehension at all, who started racing by buying his own Bentleys before he joined the team.

In 1928, Woolf Barnato and Bernard Rubin covered 1,658 miles in the 4½ to win. It was a good year for British entrants as a whole: the little Alvis entrants both broke the 1500 cc record for the race and the Lagonda team, despite two of the cars crashing into one another, managed to complete the 24 hours (in the case of the car driven by Baron d'Erlanger and Douglas Hawkes) with a broken frame and ineffectual front brakes.

The marvellous year: 1929. Barnato and Birkin in first place in a 6½,

Quite a number of Bentleys gain a sobriquet by association with a particular owner or exploit. This car is known as the Forrest-Lycett 8. It was built by L C McKenzie from a 2½-ton Corsica-bodied car. He reduced both the weight (to about 33 cwt), and the frontal area, dramatically. At the age of 74, Forrest-Lycett drove the car to regain his Belgian speed record at over 140 mph

– Old Number One – Lt. Cmdr Glen Kidston and Clive Dunfee second, Benjafield and the Baron d'Erlanger third, Frank Clement and Monsieur J Chassagne fourth, all in 4½-litre Bentleys – with the 8-litre Stutz nowhere. And the French? 'C'est une honte' commented Charles Faroux, the greatest authority on French motoring, quoted as such gleefully in Bentley's own commemorative publication; 'It's a disgrace! I am ashamed of my own country.'

Victory for the fourth successive time in 1930; Big Sixes first and second – Woolf Barnato again triumphant and in the same car as the previous year – two Talbots and an Alfa-Romeo trailing in their wake. 75.87 mph was the winning average speed. Bentley entered six cars to beat off what was seen by many as the main challenge from Rudolf Caracciola in a supercharged Mercedes. There were two Bentley teams that year, one the Bentley Motors victors and the other the Bentley Blowers led by Tim Birkin and backed by the Hon. Dorothy Paget. Tim Birkin's supercharged 4½ was clocked at 126 mph down the Mulsanne straight. The tar on the course melted in the heat, and so did the Blower Bentleys, just as W O had predicted.

1930 was the end of the line for the Bentley race team at Le Mans, and the supercharged 4½s also withdrew from racing altogether, following further not unsuccessful efforts at the French Grand Prix at Pau and at the 500.

Whilst racing for Bentley will always be Le Mans, the cars have a venerable record at Brooklands, including the six-hour endurance 'mini-Le Mans' initiated by Benjafield and Davis, and the Double-Twelve, as close to the French race as it was possible to get in Britain. Even after the last yellow flag had fallen for the marque at the Sarthes circuit, Bentleys continued to race in the hands of privateers, and as the pictures shown here demonstrate, racing rages in the Bentley blood even today.

The beautiful rust patination on the unusual body of this 4½-litre begs the perennial question: how much restoration should be done?

3-litre Le Mans model; when W O Bentley and F T Burgess designed their first car it was bought by sporting businessmen and socialites who were quite happy in the open air. As the profile of the Bentley owner changed, the cars changed accordingly. The market demanded heavy enclosed coachwork which meant longer chassis and in turn a bigger engine to compensate for all that extra weight

Racing at Silverstone; this is the handicap race, with touring models at the front. The racers have to carve their way through the pack and some cars have to make up whole laps on their slower rivals

Right, below and opposite
The most successful vintage racing Bentley of the last 20 years, YP41 was piloted by David Llewellyn for many years and is now driven by his son Tim. Racing was of course a prime motivating force in the Bentley story from the very beginning: the first win came as far back as 1921 in a junior sprint handicap (ahead of a Douglas)

Above
4½-litre special owned by Adam Stacy-
Marks. Of the 700 or so 4½s built, 55
were 'Blower' Bentleys. Aluminium
could always be specified.

Right
Definitely a competition car, as can be
seen from the feat advertised on the T-
shirts, achieved by Gordon McDonald
who set up the car for racing

Cindy Llewellyn puts 'Bluebell' through her paces at Silverstone. This is one of the most raced Bentleys around. L C McKenzie acquired the car in 1936 and shortened the wheelbase to 9 ft $9\frac{1}{2}$ in. The Llewellyns have had the car since 1978

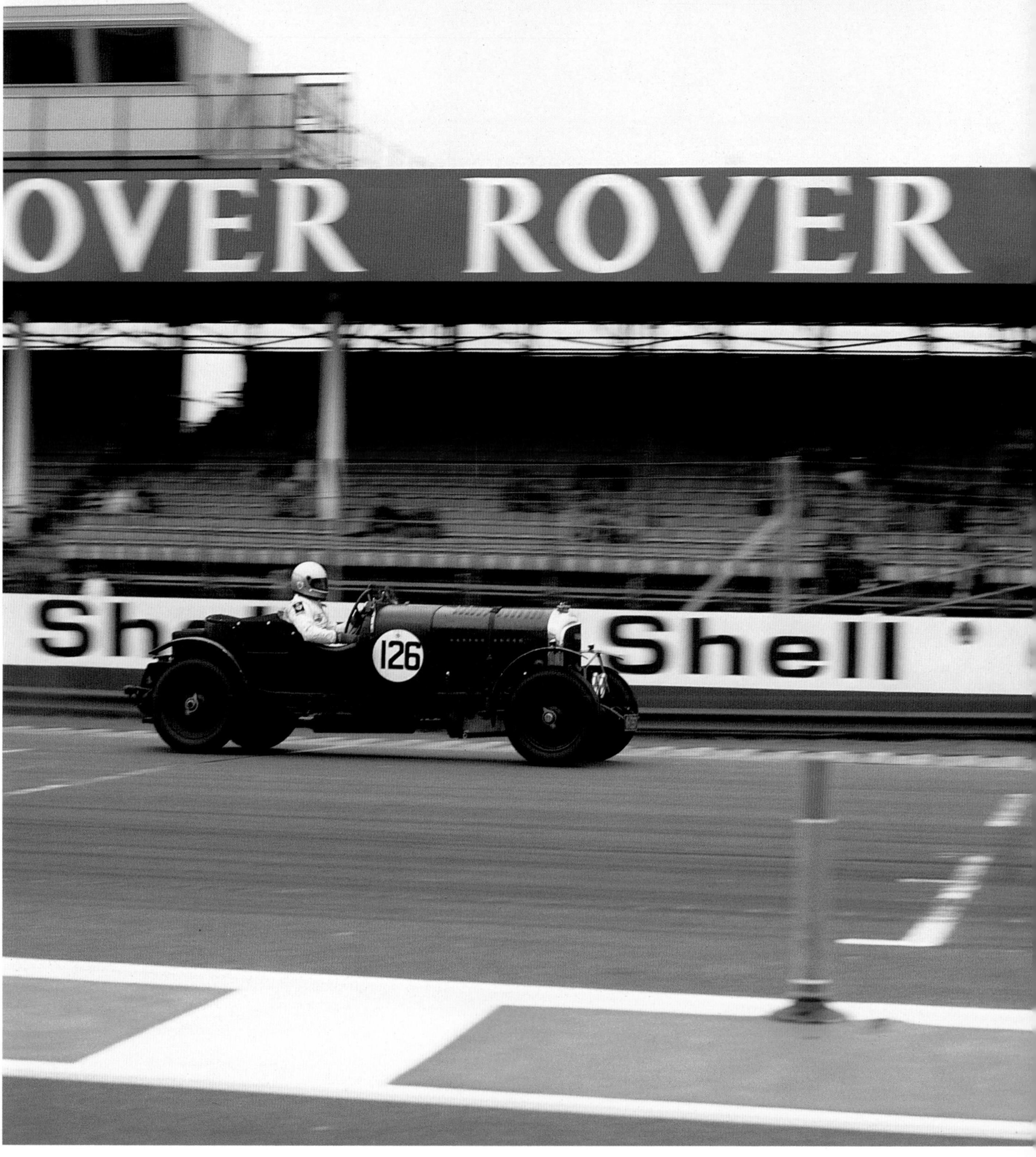
OVER ROVER
Shell
126

Left
*John Guppy enjoying himself in a 4½;
John is one of the best preparers of a
racing Bentley in the world*

Above
*'O.L.' as she is known, designed and
built by David Lewellyn, has
undergone extensive modification
before and during her ownership by
Harvey Hine, not the least of which
was the change from a 3-litre to a 4½-
litre engine. Not only a superb
competition car, but in road trim a
very fast tourer*

Above
Gibbs Pancheri's 4½ with a full family load, about to go out onto the Silverstone track

Right
Genuine Le Mans team car and owner David Vine. In the second Le Mans race of 1924 the rules stated that at the end of their fifth lap all drivers of open cars had to pull into the pits and erect the hood. After twenty more laps they were obliged to return to the pits for checking; any equipment fault would lead to 'instant disqualification'. Though this Speed Six never had to go through all that bother

Left
Bentley traffic jam; Mulsanne Turbo on the right, in the midst of some of the cars that suggested its name following their exploits on the Sarthes circuit back in the 1920s

Above
The following pictures are of genuine Le Mans team cars. This 1925 3-litre has covered thousands of miles of hard motoring. In 1925, the so-called Le Mans start was introduced, with drivers running across the road to start their cars. No Bentley managed to finish that year

Right and overleaf
A unique body style to comply with Le Mans regulations. This 1926 100-mph car was the only 9-ft wheelbase 3-litre to run at Le Mans

1927 3-litre; the year of the spectacular crash involving three Bentleys, and of victory for the second time. Much of the coachwork has of course changed, but the chassis is still there. The car crashed after $5\frac{1}{2}$ hours, which spelt the end of its racing career. This piece of Bentley and Le Mans history now resides in the suitably elegant city of Bath

Left

1928 4½-litre. Around dawn on 17 June at Le Mans, the frame cracked and the flexing pulled off a radiator hose, which meant retirement. The 4½ which actually won the race also cracked its frame. All long chassis Bentleys were henceforth reinforced and fitted with underchassis braces

Above

This and one other car specially prepared for Le Mans received an unusual rear-end treatment to house the spare wheel, thus earning the nickname 'Bobtail'

Left

A door enabled the racers to check the oil level and top up without having to open up the bonnet; anything to save seconds in the pits

Bill Lake is the fortunate owner of this 1930 Speed Six

Above
Cockpit of the Speed Six. The 1930 Le Mans tended to bear out W O's objections to supercharging: the Hon. Dorothy Paget's team Blower Bentleys failed to finish, as did the supercharged Mercedes

Right,
This Speed Six won the Double Twelve at Brooklands on 9/10 May, 1930. On 21/22 June, it finished second at Le Mans

Opposite above
Speed Six powerplant; the model wasn't just successful in the French classic. Barnato and Dunfee won the British Automobile Racing Club six hours race at Brooklands in June 1929 in a Speed Six; and the model gained a one-two in the Double Twelve the following year

Opposite below
Off-side view, showing the second ignition system and its linkage

Above and right
Second in the Double Twelve at Brooklands in May 1930, this Speed Six DNF at Le Mans a few weeks later. Clive Dunfee crashed into a huge sandbank at Pontlieue corner and practically buried the car. He tried for two hours to dig it out; then co-driver Sammy Davis left the pits to give it a shot, digging away with a headlamp glass, to no avail

Above

The white paint on the wing was to help the pit crew to identify the cars during the Le Mans; Bentley no. 2, GF 8507, was painted on the off-side wing, no. 4 had no marker; simple but effective

Right

The roar from that exhaust and the whine from the supercharger of the challenging Mercedes must have sounded like the end of the world with both cars flat out down the Mulsanne straight

A piece of Brooklands (and Bentley) history; this is the Bentley Jackson Special, sometimes known as the Marker Jackson. Robin Jackson built the car on his own chassis design in 1936/37 for owner Richard Marker, who lapped the Brooklands track at 134.97 mph. That kind of speed put the car at the top of its class

The Bentley Jackson was rebuilt from the chassis up in the Stanley Mann workshops from parts which owner Vaughan Davis (giving instructions to the driver) had had for many years

The awesome 24-litre Napier aero-
engined Bentley; three banks of four
cylinders with aircraft stub exhausts.
Napier nearly secured the services of
W O back in 1932, before Rolls-Royce
stepped in

On the left, Jim Medcalf's 8-litre limousine; on the right, 3-litre Le Mans superstar; centre, Diana Barnato, daughter of Woolf Barnato — another Le Mans superstar — winner in 1928, 1929 and 1930

*The spectacular 8-litre limousine out
on the circuit; Diana Barnato along for
the ride. W O himself ran an 8-litre*

Restoration – and some Ageless Stars

Left and above
Len Wilton started out with a kind of obsession: the Bentley story that inspired him was that of Old Number Seven in the 1927 Le Mans. After $5\frac{1}{2}$ hours, the famous crash damaged the off-side front wing, and, perhaps most importantly, bent the right-hand dumbiron which put the axle out of parallel. Despite this, the car won, 212 miles ahead of its nearest rival. Len Wilton spent five years reproducing the car exactly as it was on June 18, 1927, with the help of many specialists and as many of the original parts as he could obtain

The following pictures give some idea of the meticulous work of the professional Bentley restoration specialists and of the efforts of the amateur enthusiast. As previously mentioned, the uniqueness of every Bentley, which is the result of the old division between the car company and the coach builder, leaves the field wide open for the restorer. The degree of restoration is very much a question of personal preference. Many Bentleys, for example, sport the racing green so closely associated with Le Mans. (Apart from the 1924 winning car, which was painted black, the rest of the Le Mans team Bentleys were different shades of green.) But the original production models could be seen with polished aluminium bonnets, scarlet wings, duo-tone bodies in blue and black, green and brown, blue and maroon, etc. There is no good reason why any model under restoration should not don such peacock finery.

One thing that is quite obvious from any visit to the professional workshops is that the experts at work there consider Bentley restoration as a labour of love. Stanley Mann, as these photographs show, is not merely a professional restorer, he is an enthusiast who races Bentleys himself.

The final pictures in this book are a gallery of Bentley stars: that is to say, cars which have a particular historical significance, either through their owners or their racing exploits. Perhaps the most satisfying point to bear in mind when admiring these superb examples of WO's genius is that every one of them is still on the road.

More than 20 years after completion, Len Wilton is ready to renew the attempt to attain absolute authenticity, armed with new research and photographs

This Bentley is no museum piece; with 150,000 miles on the clock, the general health and look of the car is a credit to the many craftsmen who worked on it

Left
This 4½ was at the Dick Moss workshop for general maintenance. The car was rebodied at some stage, probably by Jack Barclays, in this 1930s style. Does anyone out there know for sure?

Above
4½ Le Mans 'replica' at the Stanley Mann workshop. Stanley's mascot, 'Benjafield' – named after Dr J D Benjafield, a 1920s driver and one-time owner of Old Number Seven – is in the driver's seat

Above
A very unusual and very beautiful woodgrained body in the Ivan Dutton workshop

Right
A standard late-1929 $4\frac{1}{2}$ undergoing complete restoration and gaining a supercharger at the same time. A dummy bulkhead is being built in to give extra length to the bonnet

4½-litre Le Mans receiving some final touches from Mark Bradnum at Stanley Mann

A recent restoration much influenced by the Le Mans 3-litre, with a light Vanden Plas body, quick-action radiator cap, two-stick hood and racing tyres

Above
The following photographs were taken at Stanley Mann in Radlett, Mecca for Bentley enthusiasts. Not all the cars are for sale. This is a late twenties $4\frac{1}{2}$ with folding head. The pram irons are particularly fine

Right
The helmet wings on this model are unusual; rope-bound steering wheel, racing bonnet straps and racing green are all part of the restoration

*An unusual rear end treatment,
reminiscent of Eddy Hall's mid-1930s
TT car*

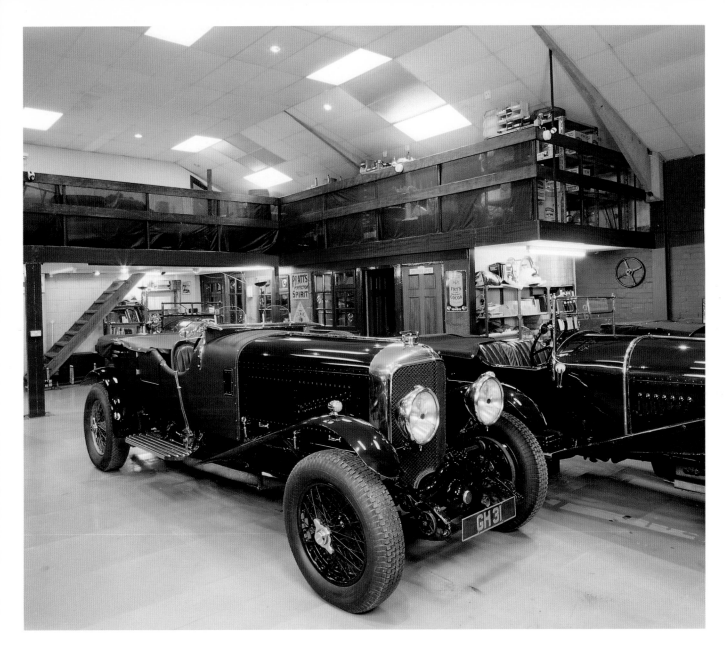

Left
The Spitfire is a reminder that W O designed aero-engines (notably for the Sopwiths) before he designed cars. Note the wire screens on lamps and grille – for the continental tour, perhaps – on this Speed Six. (1912 Blackburn Monoplane, right)

Above
Long wings and varnished wood running boards on this 1928 Bentley; some were aluminium

Overleaf
This is a very standard looking car; the tonneau cover isn't taut and from this and by the look of those seats, it probably has the original upholstery, well maintained down through the years

Left and above
GY 3904 has undergone several transformations in its lifetime, starting off with an Amherst Villiers supercharger, losing it, and then regaining supercharging at the Stanley Mann workshops. Note the massive reinforcements at the front of the car to take the blower. Michael McCormick, Workshop Manager, ensures that the detailing of the dash is exact

Fabulously elegant 6-litre at Coys the auctioneers. Note the discs covering the wire wheels. The auxiliary lamps mark this as a tourer. The upholstery on this car, obviously, has been perfectly restored. You can almost smell it

114

Left

YV 9608 was built shortly after the war from the chassis up by Tom Padden. During the war, Tom Padden served in the Royal Navy: after being torpedoed (not for the first time) he spent six weeks drifting in an open boat, during which time the design was finalised!

Above

Gordon Russell of Elmdown Vintage Autos had this car adapted when arthritis made it difficult for him to drive his Bentleys; with easy access doors, power steering and an 8-litre engine to reduce gear changing. Gear changes on vintage cars like these are a very different matter to today's tolerant machinery. Original buyers liked to know how quickly they could shift into top

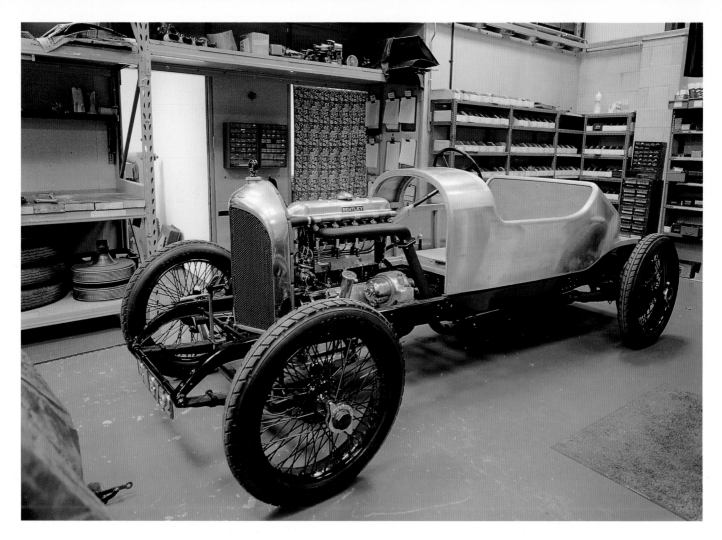

Previous page
A court case was necessary to establish that this car be known as 'Old Number One', and that the honour stay with the car despite many changes. This particular manifestation was as the car looked when it went over the top of the banking at Brooklands. The original Old Number One won the 1930 Le Mans. Its last race (and victory) was the 1931 BRDC 500 at Brooklands

Above
An historically extremely important Bentley receiving due care and attention at Elmdown Vintage Autos, Experimental Number 2; much of the development work was done on this car to produce the original 3-litre

Right
This car was first registered to Sir Henry ('Tim') Birkin in February 1927, one of the legendary 'Bentley Boys'. It was entered in the Essex Car Club Six Hours race at Brooklands on May 7 of that year. Despite losing the spare wheel and third gear, the car came third

YE 6029

Above
This venerable old Bentley has a
wonderfully original feel to it; it also
has its own place in the Bentley story,
as the car owned by Clive Gallop who
worked on the original 3-litre
camshaft. He was taken on partly
because of W O's admiration for his
work on the pre-war Peugeot

Right
Prepared by John Guppy at Stanley
Mann, this standard Speed Six took
the UK Class B (5000–8000 cc) 200-
mile standing start record at
Millbrook with an average speed of
102.3 mph – on 30 May, 1988! The
drivers were Vaughan Davis and
Stanley Mann

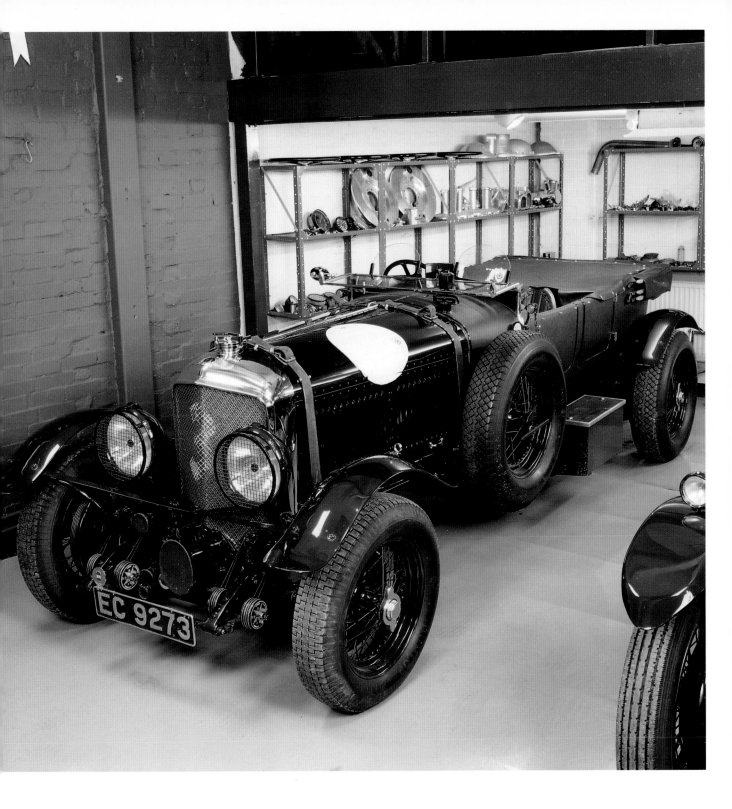

Previous page and above
Another winner prepared by John Guppy (and Stanley Mann's personal transport), this time in the UK A category, for cars over 8000 cc. To quote just a couple of examples – confirmed RAC figures – on May 29, 1989, 50 km at 122.80 mph, on October 8 the same year, five miles at an average speed of 135.36 mph. Vaughan Davis and Stanley Mann display a few trophies

This car once belonged to Woolf Barnato, winner of Le Mans on three consecutive occasions and Chairman of the Bentley company in its latter years. It is good to see that the present owner is having the saloon body restored (by Dick Moss). So many saloons have been converted to open tourers that the original closed body styles are becoming quite scarce

The chassis and axles of this saloon are from the first 4½-litre, known at Bentley Motors as the 25/100 or no. ST 3001 and later as 'Old Mother Gun'. The car won Le Mans in 1928, Bernard Rubin and Woolf Barnato at the wheel, and was second the following year. It was then kept for a year as a private car by Captain Barnato